Praise for *Our Music*

These last poems by Dennis Schmitz remind us why his was a major, and utterly distinct, voice in American poetry for more than five decades. His poems are gentle, deeply intelligent, subtle, wry, and sometimes downright funny. But always, they are attentive to the sounds and rhythms of language used well—the music of poetry. As the title suggests, music is the foundation here; whether it be Mozart or Muzak, Pachelbel or pop, it plays from the opening line—"Music tells you how you feel" to the last brief stanzas—"...but at 78, I instead hear//music from/that other side—//a low thrill, some song—/familiar, more than one voice//when there is a voice,/& I begin to hum too." What a joy it is to hear Dennis Schmitz's distinctive humming, though sadly for the last time.

—Gary Thompson, author of
Broken by Water: Salish Sea Years

Nothing compares to Dennis Schmitz's unique style of poetry, marked with lines that flow with unparalleled intelligence, wit, music, and the occasional ampersand. *Our Music* is a triumph, the culmination of a lifetime's fine tuning, a collection of melodies transposed with tacit skill, in a natural tone, always in tune, with haunting precision.

—Thomas Mitchell, author of
Where We Arrive, Caribou,
The Way Summer Ends

OUR MUSIC

Published by Gunpowder Press
David Starkey, Editor
PO Box 60035
Santa Barbara, CA 93160-0035

Cover image: "Zipper, 2001" by Roger Vail. Used by permission of the artist.

ISBN-13:978-1-957062-03-7

www.gunpowderpress.com

Our Music

Poems

Dennis Schmitz

Foreword by
David Starkey

Gunpowder Press • Santa Barbara
2022

To our father's many friends and readers.

With gratitude,
the Schmitz Family

We would like to offer special thanks to
Robin Magowan and the Magowan Family Foundation,
Gary Thompson, Susan Kelly-DeWitt, and Roger Vail for
their generous support in bringing this project to fruition.

FOREWORD

When I was growing up in the working-class northeast corner of Sacramento in the 1960s and 70s, poetry was almost entirely absent from my life and the lives of the people I knew. The only contemporary lyrics we encountered were in rock songs, and the poetry we read in school was from another era, if not another world.

The irony, of course, is that during this time, Dennis Schmitz, one of America's smartest, nimblest and most daring poets was writing and teaching at nearby Sacramento State. I should probably say *faraway* Sac State, as the university seemed so distant from Foothill High, where almost no one I knew was planning to attend college.

I was one of the lucky ones, landing at UC Davis, all the way on the other side of the Yolo Causeway, where I soon fell in love with and majored in creative writing. Years passed, during which time I, too, became a poet and professor of creative writing. So, late though it was—probably sometime in the mid-1990s, when I was living and teaching in Illinois, an important place for Dennis—I still experienced a kind of joy in discovering that a poet of such talent and reputation had been, and still was, writing poetry in Sacramento, poetry that my teenaged self would have cherished.

Of course, my tangential relation to the poet is nothing like that of the thousands of students and fellow poets whose lives Dennis touched. For them, and for his loving family, the poems in this book will be reminders of his humor, poignance, learning and outright genius. Whether we knew the man or not, we are lucky, indeed, to have his book, the publication of which is due in no small part to the efforts and enthusiasm of Dennis's son, Paul.

Our Music is the second collection in Gunpowder Press's California Poets Series, which features new volumes by important poets from the Golden State. Susan Kelly-Dewitt's *Gatherer's Alphabet* was our first book in the series, which soon include volumes by Sandra McPherson and Gary Soto. We anticipate that these, and future, books of poetry will represent an important contribution to California letters.

David Starkey
Publisher & Co-editor
Gunpowder Press

ACKNOWLEDGEMENTS

Grateful acknowledgement to the editors of the journals in which these poems first appeared, sometimes in earlier versions:

Arroyo: "Red"

Choice: "Mothball Fleet," "1971"

Cloudbank: "Bad Dog!," "My Hands," "Amorosi's Dog," "Antarctica," "The Way Back," "80ᵗʰ Birthday," "Storm Warnings," "Raccoons in the Attic," "Blessed Are Those Whose Sins Are Forgiven"

December: "Main Street," "My Eden," "Chateau D'If"

Field: "Hunger," "Counting," "The Other Side," "Lies," "Systems," "Ghosts," "The Thought-Proof Parts"

Great River Review: "Crawlspace"

Hubbub: "Two-Beer Ethics," "Writing Poetry," "Shadow-Pain"

Marsh Hawk Review: "Artistic Integrity," "New York"

Miramar: "Half Moon Bay," "Steinway," "Toothache"

New Letters: "Driving"

River Styx: "Digging Up Polemic Root"

Suisun Valley Review: "The Shaming of the Egg-Thief"

Waymark: "The Same War," "Oz," "Your Name Here," "Bucket List," "Hiding in Order to Be Seen," "The Man-Faced Beast from the Book of Kells"

CONTENTS

I.

Our Music 15

Ghosts 16

Amorosi's Dog 17

Two-Beer Ethics 18

Chateau D'If 19

Your Name Here 21

Driving 22

Antarctica 24

Shadow-Pain 25

The Shaming of the Egg-Thief 27

Hiding in Order to Be Seen 28

The Thought-Proof Parts 29

Snail Cookies 30

Raccoons in the Attic 31

Nebraska 32

Bucket List 33

The Man-Faced Beast from the Book of Kells 34

Blessed Are Those Whose Sins Are Forgiven 36

Writing Poetry 37

II.

Bad Dog! 41

Artistic Integrity 42

New York 43

Day-Help 44

My Hands 45

Lies 46

Cycling   47
Storm Warnings   48
San Francisco VA Medical Center   49
Digging Up Polemic Root   50
Oz   51
Systems   52
80TH Birthday   53
General Science   54

III.

Red   57
Fish-Talk   58
Sun   59
Main Street   61
Hunger   62
Counting   63
Insomnia   64
My Eden   65
Sin   66
Half Moon Bay   67
Mothball Fleet, 1971   68
My Benares   69
The Way Back   71
Steinway   72
Toothache   73
The Same War   74
Crawlspace   75
The Other Side   76

About the Poet   77

I.

Our Music

Music tells you how you feel,
but lyrics alone can't talk you through

a bad day. So we sigh & foot-tap
in the express-check. So we pray over

the moving belt that the toilet-paper stays
virginal, that the shrink-wrapped meat

won't squirt red or go animal again
in the long wait. Check-out or death—

whichever comes first. Overhead,
the store-music struggles for climax,

but we go on finishing bouts
of flu, or naming the babies of the next

generation.

Ghosts

By *ghost* I mean a scrap of Beethoven
or Pachelbel's "Canon" reduced to a phone's
ring-tone—a kind of musical acid reflux.

                    * * *

I mean that memory is disjunctive—
it's quoted speech, little damns.
It will give favorite clothing
to Goodwill then drive to buy it back.

                    * * *

In real life, Maria Callas
suffered like the Tosca I'd take out,

three discs to an opera, scratched,
the emotions so used that there was little music

left. Only eighteen, hearing the pain
but not the art of using it—when I tried to sing

only the Italian of it, intercepting,
ghosting over her lover's reply—

whose voice was it?

Amorosi's Dog

Like Crawford's Walt or David's black
lab, wag-less, Amorosi's dog is stranded

in death—the dog's only exercise is moving
back & forth in e-mails until I mentally run
her on Oakland hills, run until she confuses

my mind with hers, & we're both
off-leash at Berkeley Marina that's still loose
fill & tidelands, thirty years after

the Loma Prieta earthquake shifted freeways,
locking SF & East Bay in a brief

shudder, shoving the massive
upper roadway of the Bay Bridge sideways.
All the way west,
over SF, the sun's a bruise in the fog.

                    * * *

I'm running the distance between
dog & human. If dog & Fault

are paired in discontinuous movement,
does a virtual dog weigh enough to start the shake
of liquefied fill—the frantic dump-loads of old building
materials, boards never un-nailed, pavement wrapped
in snapped, useless rebar?

Two-Beer Ethics

Suppose, Tanaka argues, a school-bus—
kids. Behind the bus-glass you see the stew

of heads & sweatered elbows & a necessary
driver in his own square of glass, & give him,

for spite, snowmelt on a county blacktop.
Tanaka by now has the fly trapped inside

his bar glass against which, half-wet, it bats
fumes. Tanaka is Aristotle, he's the Angel

Moroni—he knows I won't argue two-beer
ethics, but he makes the children anyway

& supposes the snow, & out of High Street's
turns he brings the bus to the hypothetical

old woman crossing illegally as the bus
downshifts into Tanaka's icy county road.

To save the children, he says, the driver hits
the old woman—the driver intends to save

the children so it's fine to hit the old woman,
but maybe the driver shouldn't take joy

in hitting her—intention saves the driver
moral dereliction, Tanaka says, & lifts the glass

away from the fly he didn't intend to drink.

Chateau D'If

is a prison anyone can escape
   just by closing the book,
but, squinting, I steer
   THE COUNT OF MONTE CRISTO

into the boathouse window's ragged light—
   it's the library Dumas
with the deckled pages, so many times renewed

that the book is on my mother's card.
Edmund Dantes is already years
   in his cell—newer rats answer

to his false friends' names.
   I've had measles, mumps,
fourth grade—I've had every other kid's summer
of polio scare, & now this prison

is McCloskey's abandoned
& rotting boathouse. Around me, the river lifts
   the boathouse & lets go,

   continual in little splashes where
my friends exit the river, one by one, onto the warped,
&, though we've swept with somebody's shirt,
   dirt-crunchy flooring. August,

   & I have a broken arm—
the plaster cast is scribbled with the French words
for riches Monte Cristo needed to need

when he pretended death, & the guards threw
his wrapped body into the novel's next part.
The rest of the summer is there if I could swim to it.

Your Name Here

His face says that whatever he fights
fights back. His sign says he capitulates

only to you as he sits down
opposite. Does YOUR NAME HERE

on the sign mean that he expects to trade
guilt or only tell you that he begs

better with narrative, that his sign
pasted to a board & strung

over his shoulders means to emphasize
his splendidly-ratty wardrobe?

A prop, he says, an insinuation,
like the shopping-cart's wirey body

knotted with bags of cans. He says
even stale bread may be *fraught* with raisins—

something you might have said.
Are you mocking me? you say.

Are you mocking me? he says.

Driving

Forgive the body its mechanical
failures, the breakdowns; forgive

its tendency to steer itself
into other bodies. When the body

dies, its driver exits, turning off the key.
A wife or husband who's left now

sees the navel is machine-punched,
sees how the beloved's body stitchery

has leaked a few kapok shreds.
The two kids left, of course, cry.

A married aunt will take them,
will drive them to the end of her life

without accusation—
neglect sometimes equals apology,

the side-road dissolves to prickly
grass. The orphaned girl, woman now,

body quilted with fat, recalls—
or the boy in an automatic sideways

sway on his mattress over the outline
of his smaller, younger self (he's

still in the 3ʳᵈ floor room his cousin
slept in) speaks, drags a voice over

the corpse-world, the withered voice
of memory.

Antarctica

The sled dog ate my homework—
real explorers will eat their boot-laces

& finally their dogs.
What can a third-grade geography know?

Little daily snow, but centuries of it—
a few text-book traces flake

into his sleep—only child, & dog-less,
& at the half-doze, how does an eight year-old

suppose Antarctica—a continent that cracks
off in bedroom-sized pieces?

So, in the classroom, the teacher calls
him back—where has he been?

Scott says that he knew the other explorers
in the cold by their heat-haloes

& that at the end, he said, when they were few
in the ragged tent, but he counted them anyway

for his journal, & always there was one extra,
not death, but a dark boy-sized figure.

Shadow-Pain

This seventy year-old body
is the fulsome shadow that younger

body threw, & these thigh-spasms
surface over the ache of that boy's knee

the last part of my morning run.
Then, we went down like chickens

hypnotized to distract
them from the axe by drawing a line

in the dust in front of their beaks—
we touched our noses to the coach's

chalk-line exactly one foot ahead,
training with push-ups, with isometric

tension drills until our teenage
bodies concentrated the shadows,

the fats & loose sugar-flesh that the coach
mocked (Farney broke his nose

on the gym-floor when he couldn't
hold his body extra push-ups).

Bad knees & wrong-way ankles—
each teen practice is still in *this* body,

each pain blends on dark,
the death, the shadow-increase I hypnotize

myself to carry the last part of my run.

The Shaming of the Egg-Thief

as the Pusateri's clerk caught
him, shaking open
the man's coat to deliberately smash

the stolen eggs against him—
it was the summer of fourth grade,

which, I dimly knew, only flowed one way
to the harder summers of adulthood.
I knew baseball rules; I thought then that

I got the moral outcomes of movies
to the degree that now,
in the present, I could play myself

in the movie version of the Pusateri's drama,
my feelings magnified by the make-up

that would make me a boy again—anything to heal
the wrong. Who in the drama really
committed the crime, an anomaly, so that,

in a movie's kind of time-warp,
the trees in the park have devolved to leafy sticks

& garden chips, that our little river is trickling
away with entitlements & the many flushes
of rental housing, & Pusateri's itself in the present

is ironically reduced to a 7-11 or Kwik Stop?

Hiding in Order to Be Seen

He's a set of ears & connecting forehead—
the new neighbor across the yard—
        hiding in order to be seen, forfeiting
a face-width of his own privacy to look
over the window-box he must've made

        just this afternoon—he's all
glances, as his smile blooms over the undeveloped
greens—how much he's like
        Ted, our 1960s friend, self-imprisoned,
who grew then-illegal marijuana in his tiny apartment's

lit-up but only closet. I'd wonder which revealed
Ted more—the loss of choice
in what he wore, or the secret he advertised
        in his grin.

The Thought-Proof Parts

When I used to run tired,
exhausting any role to get through

each segment of the Saturday
workout—confusing the body,
counting off the wood-lot on County B,

losing count at scrub trees,
& under old oaks, the berry-canes

that grab nylon—I'd go on
assembling the little I knew
of deer as I ran, losing first, if I could,

the thought-proof parts.
I'd always turn back into myself

at the abandoned cabin—
gravel underfoot meant
I was at human ruins—the porch sliding

into an overgrown cellar-hole.
Then I'd always have some fence

until I was released to follow a trickle,
a seasonal watercourse that would find
the river whose wind-polished

surface would shine in pieces through the trees.

Snail Cookies

An hour into the car-trip, the five year-old
& I find the game he can't lose—*snail*

cookies I say (for their crunch).
& because its crust never stops crawling,

he counters with *worm*
pizza—I never can out-gross my grandson's

invention of weird foods.
Congruent but silly for both our sakes,

I give up hour after hour of scenic Oregon
coast that slides by on the window glass.

One horizon is stitched shut with pines—
the other horizon is ocean. Counting car colors,

fruits & vegetables by the alphabet—
we share miles more of car-games—by turns each

of us makes the other.

Raccoons in the Attic

Do they nest the way we do in bills,
receipts, the old tax records that I push

through our shredder, restless like we are
in our bed below them, their love-life

also an improbable five-star on Yelp?
Every night, we take turns, no snacks,

no reading, shredding sleep to listen,
so quiet ourselves that we may not even exist

for them, or, maybe in the way that
at such a distance space only implied it,

Pluto again became a planet.

Nebraska

Hitch-hiking was how I acted out
my Kerouac—I was twenty & bored

most of two days & Nebraska seemed
the same field repeating itself

horizon to horizon, & I was only
halfway back to Chicago—two days

of heat & the stink of alfalfa-pellet
refineries. I begged that first driver

to roll down a window for us to breathe.
My longest ride asked me if the glove-box

pistol told me what a threat he was
until I reminded him that Jesus died

for both of us as the man himself
had said fifteen miles before, & that

I felt already saved by his instruction.
Another driver had one hand that always

wanted intimacies—Nebraska lasted
& lasted, but was so flat & ironically easy

to exit as the rodeo-rider's mother-in-law
in the back seat with me & the grand-baby

remarked that you drop a nickel in Scott's
Bluff, & it would roll to Kansas.

Bucket List

Old age itself is like the four days
up Kilimanjaro the slick brochures show—
 you train for it, you plan
an afterlife like the Catholics promise,

you try to interpret the leopard
frozen at the summit, the summit

 Hemingway shot himself for
his failure to reach. It's like the irony
of my brother who trained for the breath-
 depriving climb to Machu Picchu

but not the cancer that killed him
first. How do you cross to death

 when the body is no longer a bridge
over the mind's discontinuity,
when memory is just another muscle

in spasm? Like your cousin who came
back from death said that at the end

 there was no fabled light ahead,
no regeneration suffusing the body—
that the summit was only rocky dirt
like the earth below. Two company bearers

had to carry him his last steps.

The Man-Faced Beast from the Book of Kells

The ant's ecto-skeleton defines scope
& ant-mind at the same time:

the ant never can grow to the monster
of science-fiction movies.

The clerk at the Downtowner Hotel
could bench-press 200 lbs,

or, he says, one whiskery dead-beat—
the clerk's limits, as he rattles

your room's metal-sheathed door
(a kind of ecto-skeleton)

to wake you, insistent, are still human.

* * *

The Irish monks squinted almost
to blindness to make The Book of Kells.

At the museum, bewildered by codices,
illuminations & enameled, chitinous Bible

covers, their colors a mineral evolution,
you warm yourself all Free Tuesday.

Your epiphany is less: your yellow jacket
is unzipped to the dozen rings you'd pinned

in the lining; in the left sleeve, your arm
is almost inflexible with wristwatches

you'll peddle down bus aisles or to commuters
on my Evanston train. At the exhibit case,

guard alert, you fingerprint the glass & look
at the Bible version—who can care what

the Book of Kells *says*, but only for process,
against which Matthew's gospel speaks,

describing the man possessed of demons
who are condemned to go down in swine—

academics adore even the flecked old ink itself,
neurasthenic bugs crushed for the text's color.

Blessed Are Those Whose Sins Are Forgiven

said the Bible card I tried to pass
back to a proselytizing woman on the BART
train because I felt already blessed—
my breakfast secured, the sun wavering

but persuadable above the East Bay
fog—so why was I annoyed
by her social fault & not my sin?

       * * *

Weeks later, at the Pigeon Point Lighthouse,
I knelt to look where a kneeling volunteer dug
up prohibited non-native plants & grasses
from sand the nearby ocean pulled
the other way with tidy, white-rimmed waves—

the volunteer was quoting somebody as she lifted
from one huge interlaced pile of dying
ice-plant, African daisies, their white
roots so unnaturally long, so inter-knotted—how the plants

cling to this life, she apologized, asking if it was a sin
to be planted in the wrong
places, to live out your flowering
under a foreign sun?

Writing Poetry

Just use the carpenter's rule: *measure
twice, cut once.* & twice still will leave

my father's older brother,
Uncle-the-Priest, his black Ford

improvising a road to us
through the Iowa snow.

> * * *

Put his Roman collar on the kitchen
table where he would, its power

shorting out against the metal.
I was a boy—I briefly dared the collar

around my own throat.

> * * *

Our poetry will make him sing,
his baritone reduced to a mew

by cancer—musical scraps my mother
hated but pounded out for him

on the Wurlitzer, the wool spats
he wore against 1940's Iowa

winter drying on a radiator.
I learned Latin from scraps of English

penciled by him in his broken-
backed Latin text of Horace, writing

this, the only poetry that he could,
all the long years of country rectories.

II.

Bad Dog!

Loudly, & in the busy Safeway lot—
a woman scolding her tiny Pomeranian—

did the three-headed & thus indecisive
Cerberus, as other dogs do, also pee-mark

the limits of Hades? Inconsolable Conan
Doyle, a doctor but self-infected with quackery,

tried with spiritualists to bring back
from Hades just the voice of his dead son.

My own son was inconsolable when we denied
him a dog—the landlord wouldn't permit pets.

A few days later, I admitted that we owned
the house & were ourselves the landlords

from Hades! Doyle's vengeful hound
of the Baskervilles, the extreme form of family dog—

Doyle outlined its bite in phosphorus. Doyle
won't tell what kept the Baskerville heir sleepless—

the glow or fangs of in-bred madness? That he was
the last Baskerville? Even Sherlock Holmes,

too solitary to be lonely, kept a Watson
as his pet & toothless critic.

Artistic Integrity

Mailer had thanked me when I returned THE NAKED
AND THE DEAD a hundred pages shorter—for years

integrity meant postponing someone else's fame.
It meant at writers' retreats that I'd steal back

the Promethean words wrongly used—
sometimes I took the flash drives for novels,

but usually word by word I reclaimed integrity
for someone else, if only erasing a few poem-lines

from a shared computer. Use Van Gogh's ear
as a love-token (he did), not in a quarrel

about integrity. I'm not Hitler's Eichmann, confessing
somebody else did it—I stole TYPHOON'S MISTRESS

from your agent's mail-drop; I made it confetti.
Why did you let the rebels ravage Evita, & overplaying

the metaphor, make the typhoon re-define the slave
quarters as it wiped away the island's beauty?

Roderick's revenge too was sexually suggestive & part
of the poor taste that I've enjoyed erasing.

New York

is the muggers who won't unionize
& so work, 4 AM, the Park's Great Lawn

in rain's insistent April spritz.
New York is Manganaro's improbable

but right fennel fighting the garlic
for the glory of both—New York is transaction

& *quid pro quo* & every illusion a forfeit—
it's the way you are passed from glance

to glance the crosstown blocks to Zabar's.
New York—how could you die alone

after so much handling? Never really a New
Yorker, I'd mutate, lapse into the fleshy synthesis

of bodies in the Times Square shuttle I always took
to 42nd Street's blocks of beat-up movie theaters

like the Selwyn where late morning I once watched
what I thought was a knife-fight—maybe about

a Coke—two guys at it, cut for cut, maybe one blade
or none. But the audience, day-long dwellers, teens & drunks—

New Yorkers—urbane, eyes only on the screen,
of course choosing Art not the knife—just shifted a few

stained plush seats over from the fight.

Day-Help

Maybe I wipe your phone
number from the cubicle

wall & the inadequate outline
of your body the seated man

scratches there as his intestines
rope-burn all he ate. Or maybe

I wake you in a lobby
chair, asleep in routine

sweat. Evolution is done
when legs grow

out of the brain, when big
words are spliced to stunted

bodies. In the kitchen,
you're a glove the butcher

drops, or just generic man,
the animal God hand-shaped

from scraps. Your instincts
shrivel into fingerprints.

I wipe them away.

My Hands

Ants freckle my wrists.
One on each arm, two neighbors work

my hands, loving me but raking my hands
into the grit until blood fertilizes the dark

parallels my fingers leave.
I volunteer no song, but my neighbors' low scat

My Jesus overlaps the traffic
noise from Franklyn, the far-off Con

Edison pruning, all the city continuity
that is part of a subplot that feeds us

while the narrative goes on—our dream
of lapidary glazes on apples shined

against grass, the sun sugaring young
muscat grapes. As I dig, I bless

Laurence, the third neighbor, who digs too
at the aches in my back under the sweated-through

shirt, & bless the way the earth resists
me—a grid of dried squash runners,

the radishes wilted to thread-knots—
a drought so intense that even the spade's

shadow hardens across the dug-up ground
where an earlier digger had stepped down the blade.

Lies

Churchill used them
as *terminological*

inconsistencies.

* * *

The would-be suicide—
does the help-line

clinician use
musical notation

to record her cries?

* * *

At Delphi,
afterward, having

said it, the god
longed to have said it

clearly.

Cycling

Socially-insolvent, shy, I mentally pedal
my life everywhere—anything powered

will pass me, honking. But who plays
arbiter in the Above, whose voice

in the wind-torn trees—luck is
promiscuous, Freud somewhere

warns. Even so, I always wake
virginal & alone in bed, the tea-kettle's

low whistle knotted into the fabric
of 7 AM sounds. By 8 AM, I've highlighted

the Trumpisms I had already underlined
until the CHRONICLE's print begins to crawl.

        * * *

Soured by Trump, giving up on context,
I pedal behind the first bumper-sticker that

puzzles me. I bend to it & squint & pedal
harder to read humanity's common journey.

As I pedal toward it, the message accelerates
away, gets smaller.

Storm Warnings

Tonight the surf's at most a heavy breather
on the phone, not quite a threat, almost a whisper

like a taken-back lie, the littlest stones consenting
as waves curl around

them.

      * * *

Kim Jong-un ventured a Western-style breakfast.
The second Trump tweet was mostly pique & faux-grit.
Mr. Putin's exercise regimen went extra push-ups.

      * * *

We take off our already-wet shoes & wade.
Only a city beach—Ocean Beach—no peril,
except that which love itself makes.

San Francisco VA Medical Center

to Martha

Land's End is a location & a metaphor
for what vets can suffer—all of the US

east & the Pacific grumbling
in rocks under the hospital's cliffs.

Mostly, I have to make up what you do
from the arcana of psychology or movies

like SPELLBOUND in which wily Hitchcock
makes Ingrid Bergman an analyst—like you

a professional-but-blonde. In a second movie,
the hawk never returns, though its handler's glove

is not dirtied by earlier kills—how do you talk
a vet down from evasion, or listen past a vet's

self-maiming, listen because self-repair is an act
of conscience you can't guide, because feelings

are thoughts that leave an exit wound,
because, for a vet's healing, his enemy's wounds

must scab over.

Digging Up Polemic Root

An anthem hums under the country,
mile by mile tying Montauk to Pt. Arena

in CA with wide-awake static.
It knots around graves,

inches along in gravel, amplified
by rivers it can parallel.

We are told to dig
in shifts, even make up words by lot

to shout back as we listen,
husband & wife, to find the fault,

the source, which is returning
two sounds for every agony

we pretend. Yesterday was X,
but we found nothing—

we dug, expecting leg-bones or a secret
tooth, but we found only this wire

nothing can cut.
Someone calls a boy to press his ear

to the wire as the indignities fade.

Oz

to Martha

Spared, but in fact, re-wounded like the vets
you help—some nights Lyle's uncle was

one of the monkeys who'd rip Scarecrow open,
& some nights, he was Scarecrow stuffing

the self back in. That first year home,
he odd-jobbed a life, repairing or painting

our houses—most mornings putting himself
in the same army fatigues, sergeant's chevrons

he'd pasted to his backside where he also
instinctively wiped hands paint-stained white

or the yellow of Mrs. Kutch's airless third-floor rental.
Looking up the ladder, when Lyle poured paint

or cleaned brushes, Lyle always saw those hands
on his uncle, pushing him to climb to apotheosis—

radiant, loosely human. Lyle's uncle, so wounded
by what he had to do to the godless enemy that by

summer's end, Lyle had to finish ceilings for him, breathing
in the trapped fumes or guilt that his uncle couldn't take.

Systems

Any system works at its own suicide
its own way like our scavenged

'36 Packard my dad called *Dowager*,
or a system of endangered but inbred

plover closed off in a few acres
of Point Reyes sand. Or, system within

systems, my Berkeley neighbor planting
his Ford pick-up with nasturtiums—

hood gone, more dirt shoveled in through
the windows, the truck pretend-trucking

a bed-load of lantana & poppies uphill
into our shared driveway. Or, earlier, entropy

in my '70s Wisconsin commune. Never *wrought*
enough to be *over-wrought*, I thought why not

just turn over & dream in this fertile dark?
& why not, at night, tonight, steal one swim

more if the community pond too is a system
& the wind's underbelly dragging through

pond grass is only the story's way
to distract me from drowning?

80ᵀᴴ Birthday

I've already packed extra socks
in case there is an after-life

& let the years do their own math.
I was delivered to my mother

a leaky vessel & loud—
the nurse, I saw, was impressed,

& I was issued a childhood.
Today I re-gift your praises

as I walk in the rain that's shredded
to mist by the eucalyptus.

I praise this break in the never-done
Calif drought that still crackles

underfoot. My $30 gift shirt is wet,
my sandals slide, but I rejoice

in this birth-day of everything around me.

General Science

Their teacher preaches scale
& accuracy as the 8th grade scientists

paint the sun tennis-ball size at their school's
bus-stop, then measure out the rest

of the solar system—in a whole block
of sidewalk just a few paint-dot planets

to show the loneliness of space.
Maybe the students really want to spot

each other with paint & not explain
waste in evolution or the blackened scabs

of gum between planets, the Coke cans,
the paper scraps blowing interplanetary,

an earth-dot too small for civilizations—
but they puzzle most about the Carmen

for whom her beloved had left a worn-away
heart on the sidewalk crack near Venus.

Red

We fish the froth behind
us as the party boat's one hire scatters

his chum—heads, guts, whatever
blood it took to make fish—

in it, feathers
of the gulls fighting overhead

for it, the too-early sun
only a Band-Aid on a bad cut—

red in the froth, on our hands & over
the deck & up the wheelhouse.

Today, we're subtracted to three—
two retirees & a kid, so the Bay

is only a make-do. Just a wink
north, the Brothers Light warns

too late the one docked freighter,
already unloaded. It's a red the chum

started—none of us wants it,
but it coats us anyway.

Fish-Talk

to Stuart

My older brother taught me *carp*
is the verb to complain about it,

but the noun is only a sad-faced
bottom-feeder he couldn't make me toss

up the bank to die & purify the slough.
Perch is a dry somewhere
you sit to fish & also a more desirable

fish. Out of the dark, by Coleman
light, we supposed sharks,
sting-rays or GEOGRAPHIC's *whiskery*

rascals of the deep, the slough around
us swallowing every glimmer until we fished

by feel. We lived where our town
dwindled, where the river made it lose
its edges, where the Depression

finally ebbed & I was born, figured in
as a family dry spot, the second of two

boys.

Sun

The church volunteers bring
a reluctant 7 AM sun—its light

in the alley is like hardened
grease loosening in a hot pan,

shimmery & specked.
The volunteers' van brings

a nurse, it brings coffee & bakery
day-olds compacting in plastic bags—

jelly donuts, chocolate-on-chocolate,
glazed—whatever any of the men

would've wanted at age ten, they get now.

     * * *

The ragged first men breakfasted
already on what went last

into the dumpster, but all of them still exit
for the sun which coats them as they shuffle

coffee-ward. Sun dries them unevenly
as they line up for the nurse who is

a kind of grocery clerk, who checks
them for bruises & stone-rot.

     * * *

The degradation stops hurting—
the sun has lowered itself

into the highest windows,
exceeds whatever would dilute it,

overflows what would contain it—
the boundaries of the alley,

the well-meant failures of the volunteers.
Sun wipes color on the storefronts.

Sun spreads even with traffic mishaps,
& in the infectious joy of the pedestrians.

Main Street

Stop, I shout at the woman
but also at my two grandkids who,

back to front seat, fight to punch
radio buttons for the music they don't want

me to hear. The woman, who has crossed
against the light, doesn't stop

but only bounces against our car door.
Earbuds in, she's singing the whole playlist

of love—maybe it's only teen-pop,
a kind of musical dandruff, but her head

is in the neons. She's main-streeting
what she feels. The beat is in her strut—

Lester's Sno-Kone, boarded-over Dress-Rite
Dresses & a weedy lot in between—

none of us is in singing's neighborhood,
but the head can't help what the body wants

to do. I sing thanks with the grandkids—
in spite of groan & mental stutter, I let myself sing.

Hunger

is first premise when you argue
any eating—a hint of what the goats

must feel as this herd, dozens, eats
off a hillside above the Richmond

on-ramp where I stall in 4 PM traffic,
the freeway below spilled out

glittery & turbulent. You see the goats
working in other urban clearings,

up the East Bay ridge among houses—
selective weeders hired for star thistle

nothing can kill except by the eating
of it—spikey crown a conspicuous blue.

You can see how intent they are
in their devotions, how the goats bow,

take turns to half-kneel. Their eating
is vicarious daring when so many truths

are hard to eat. I am the kind that just
listens to whatever my car-radio

supposes. Bored, I dial through music,
wars & junk-news, maybe hungry

in my own way.

Counting

Everyone else is collecting sleep
that they are owed, the house all around you

a featureless dark. But the TV screen
is a lit doorway you go in past vampire

movies, the talk shows, to insomniac's
TV—your life played back with bad

laugh-tracks. The Bronx half-sister
who is stealing the Scarsdale boy—

split couples back together in the few
minutes of story always wedged between

commercials. Then, suddenly, it's the former
Nina from "Slow Burn," all of her snugly

in her dress, two-stepping toward you,
the dance-studio bright behind her.

She is wrinkle-less & still chirpy,
not noticing that she is in an infomercial—

as she dances, saying, that if you can count,
you can dance—dancing is the math

you failed in school, the prom queen
you never added in. Subtracted to yourself,

embarrassed to be in pajamas, you still get
up from the chair, & start to count.

Insomnia

Hours before I dissolve into sleep,
I try to float there. I am Cartesian

dualism. I control-breathe.
I count my teeth with my tongue

many times. I am the pilot
of consciousness doing a pre-flight

check: left eye—*closed*.
Right eye—*open & tracking*

but still programmed
to be only a body-part.

* * *

One night I finally read my way into
sleep or its composite & by morning

climb out sleep's other side,
shreds of prose still clinging & Prince

Andrei hours behind. Only Tolstoy & I
know Andrei is where I gave him up

in the Rostov courtyard, wounded
& spacey in a wagon-load of wounded.

A book's only a mental conveyance—
envying Andrei even his painful sleep,

I pause, then read deeper into my own dark.

My Eden

I'd try Eden first in chalk, sketching the meaning
quick like the sidewalk panels at a Sunday

street fair—easy dramas everyone
walks through, tracking *Sunset* chalk-dust

into *The Battle of Gettysburg*.
I'd have to make this world erasable

for the disaffected, for those who storm
against themselves, the wired

& weirded-out. I begin my humans
with blue chalk & let the sidewalk work

earth-colors through their flesh.
Even my animals would start out

as humans—I perfect them with fur,
elongate teeth. Of themselves, they drop

down on all fours. Aardvark, vole
to wildebeest, they all start out as Adam,

& in the Garden, chalk-stroke
by chalk-stroke, lose their human inadequacies.

I squeeze them in tight so that there is no room
for self-damnation. This world is two-dimensional,

but should I make it morally easy?

Sin

The snake, which could not
kneel, made God kneel
to make it—O contrary Eden—

is Nature the true nature,
& Adam, the merely ornery,

become the sinful,
damned to the Biblical world

in a kind of rendition?
Worst sin—My Lai, or back to
Ugolino in Dante's INFERNO

where Dante was the only one
alive & forbidden by his guide
Virgil to touch the dead or address

them except by their sins?

* * *

What about the never-tempted
who must live out their Eden

kissing rusty kisses,
their hands patrolling the limits

of touch?

Half Moon Bay

Ex-urban San Francisco but south—
the coastal fog burns off
by noon, & my own head-fog clears as I look

down, dizzy to walk every AM the same
crumbly bluffs. How high am I? How far out
my horizon? By simple geometry that

I almost remember, the horizon's seven miles
out for every thirty feet I'm up.
Mostly artichoke fields above the beach,
&, in most crab-seasons, crab-fishing

beyond that. Afternoons are
California—always summer even when
the id can't stand the joys

of ice still in a half-consumed drink,
or some shade a breeze tears from eucalyptus
to where I lie darkened by it.
Eucalyptus, like me, was an exotic,

a 19th century idea, a failure—Australian
trees so straight, but they shattered
easily—they were so-so shade trees, but worthless
even for railroad ties.

Mothball Fleet, 1971

40 years of highways unspool
over the bald hills

to the chilly summer
delta above Benicia where the only

sky still inches out of illegal
smokestacks. I remember the town's

only bait-shop. The owner, one-legged
WW II vet, hopped—too old

for the refineries, too smart
for fishing. But his flat-nosed daughter

went some Sundays with the plant
off-crews to fish the repeated

endless distortion of Liberty
ships, destroyers & a mine-tender

for sturgeon. Their skiff would circle
the sun-bleached mother

ships as their outboard noises came
back bigger from the high

sides furred with rust—water
is slow, but the years of war

must leak through.

My Benares

to Robin Magowan

was an adolescent's India—I'd go there
afternoons from the shadowy Carnegie

library, homework done, the Iowa heat
somehow redistributed through the thousands

of books—what was I once? What failure of self
engendered me? Perhaps I intuited a world

where God was a verb, not a noun,
& the Ganges was the flow of death,

that you died many times, that death wasn't
anything but your personal series of bad births.

I supposed the river pushing human ashes
not wet enough to sink—husks & fruit rinds,

garbage going gelatinous, & in the foreground,
the one man bathing splashed in joy.

This is how I supposed a Hindu transfer
of souls—the only currents were

concentric circles from the purge of bodies
dropped out of the seething & half-dressed

crowds—the crush of the living waiting
their turns, down successive stone steps

or ledges maybe a thousand years used,
shaped to bared feet & wrapped cadavers.

Crowds, but in the oily water, single bodies
making those circles, & in the atmosphere

over the river, I imagined souls clustered
like Benares pigeons let go from the highest

cupola—maybe up among the pigeons
a flight of the unborn.

The Way Back

Off-trail, trees interlaced
with fallen trees—the creek we step

across twice on the way up
is folded & re-folded into the terrain—

even the idea of creek could be
only the crease in the badly-folded

topo map Bob is now cursing.

* * *

Maybe smells I don't have a nose for
could, but looking can't tell us

the way back through all the greens
except for a ribbon, a contaminant red,

I'd tied on a branch two days before.

* * *

We're miles by a short-cut to the car,
& no matter the poncho, wet December

runs through all our cloth
layers & finally underfoot.

The trail's old & maybe made
by animals years ahead of us.

6 AM in anxiety's half-dark;
the two of us struggle & sway
up the visible into the guessed.

Steinway

to Loretta

We're tight in our too-small cottage,
but the Steinway never crowds

us as its music expands who we are.
Where are you going when you find

your way through the intricacies
of Bach—who are we this time

in our tiny rental cottage, its window-
glass flexing at the *forte* of some music

I don't know but try to hum? Even in
the kitchen, when your fingers slow

to a crawl, the pots ring back some
of the indistinct notes in you.

The Steinway is big enough to have
its own gravity—leaning into it,

your small body always trembles,
shaken even by a quiet Mozart adagio.

Toothache

to Loretta

It could be an easy metaphor for love
that makes me sleepless the whole night,

my face a mask of hurt—
is it only tooth-pain or a contrary thrill

the pain-mask won't hide when I kiss
you good-morning? 7 AM, coffee ignored,

you're already at your dog-eared
& underscored Panikkar, not really looking

at metaphors for toothache in *The Rhythm
of Being*, though immanence may be another

term for God suffusing our nerve-ends,
& pain is God touching me

on a minor nerve before I kiss through
the pain-mask to kiss you? Already, I bend my face

to interrupt your face, desperate for a second kiss.

The Same War

to Loretta

Boko Haram or the US drone-kills—
today's war is the same war
you protested by digging symbolic graves

& their crosses for Vietnam
noncombatants, & you're the same

as when history flickered
you full-face into our local news,
arrested for digging in the Federal Bldg's

lawn. In the background, a distracted cop hands
me & our arrested friends your spade & cops drag

you foreground, your face taking the whole
front page. Some brief jail was just your moment
in someone else's unfinished dying,
the Viet body-count daily posted on our front page—

what you surrendered to was not the habit
of going along, which may drag us
by fingers or loose clothing into the machine,

but moral choice.

Crawlspace

Momentarily I've lost my saw-cut
in the uncertain light, & somehow I've turned

backwards into my tool-belt, all rattles
& metal-threats, kneeling but not praying—

having lost both the crawlspace's
light string, & on the way to it, my blackened

palm-prints feeling across the attic's
one remembered wall. I'm still holding the saw,

& with the other hand flicking the sawdust
that pads my knees. My mother's father

(I called him Ernie) called each of his pockets
by the brand of sweet he hid there—jujubes,

mint discs I could pronounce, & at three or four,
I had to find in that visit's pocket as together

the two of us re-thought the sweetness
both of us hid. From one pocket he'd hold up

lint or maybe screws & metal littles
from his thumb & finger's crawlspace, a vest

pocket—sometimes he discovered a lost
pencil-end, but the candy lit by his calling forth

never did not guide his fingers.

The Other Side

The way motel walls are
so thin that you hear

the polyglot of lovers
the exchange of groans

the sleepers turning
over in the cheap beds

the late-night
flushes—there is a thin

wall between being old
& the personal death that's just

on the other side,
but at 78, I instead hear

music from
that other side—

a low thrill, some song—
familiar, more than one voice

when there is a voice,
& I begin to hum too.

About the Poet

Dennis Schmitz was born in Dubuque, Iowa in 1937 and graduated from Loras College. He then moved to Chicago to serve as a community organizer. While taking graduate courses at the University of Chicago, he decided to devote himself to writing. He taught at several colleges in the Midwest before coming to California State University, Sacramento in 1966, where he was a beloved professor of English for over thirty years. As a poet, Schmitz was known for the complexity, humanity, and humor of his work. Throughout his life, he and his wife Loretta were advocates for social justice and the environment—themes that feature prominently in his writing, alongside the Iowa riverscapes of his childhood, the working-class neighborhoods of Chicago, and the rough grandeur of the California coast. His collections include *We Weep for Our Strangeness*, *Double Exposures*, *Goodwill, Inc.*, *String*, *Singing*, *Eden*, *About Night*, *The Truth Squad*, and *Animism*. In addition, he won the di Castagnola and Shelley Memorial Awards from the Poetry Society of America, and Guggenheim and National Endowment for the Arts Fellowships. A tireless mentor to numerous writers, Schmitz's honors culminated in being named the first poet laureate of Sacramento in 1994. He died in 2019 at his home in Oakland, California.